Unit 3
Faithfulness

Deuteronomy 7:9

Joshua 1:9

Psalm 101:6

Matthew 25:23

Unit 2
Bible Study and Prayer

Psalm 119:9-11

Psalm 29:2

Hebrews 4:12

Philippians 4:6

Unit 1
Attributes of God

Psalm 103:6

Psalm 103:7

Psalm 103:8-9

Psalm 103:10

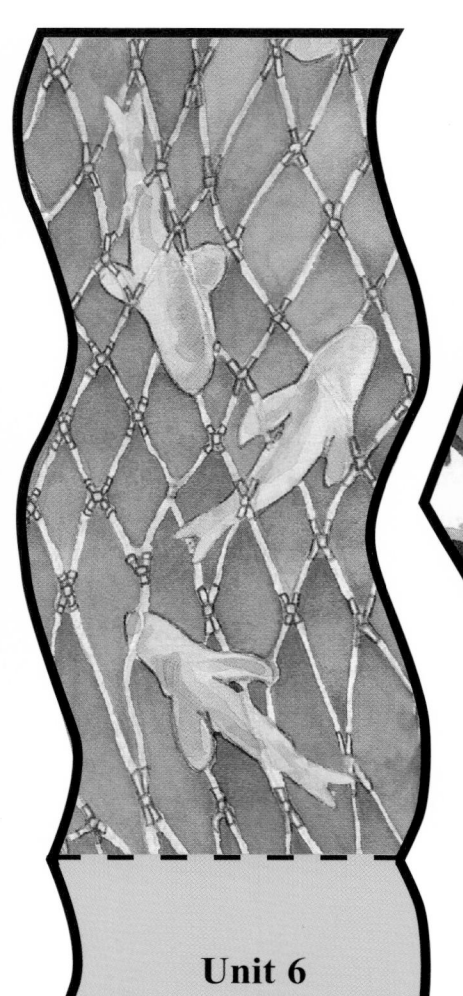

Unit 6
Contentment

Hebrews 13:5
I Timothy 6:6-8
Matthew 6:25-26
Philippians 4:11

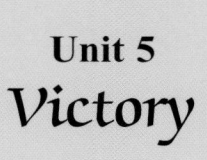

Unit 5
Victory

James 1:12-13
James 1:14-15
I Corinthians 10:13
Ephesians 2:8-9

Unit 4
Christmas: Announced by Angels

Luke 1:37-38
Luke 2:52

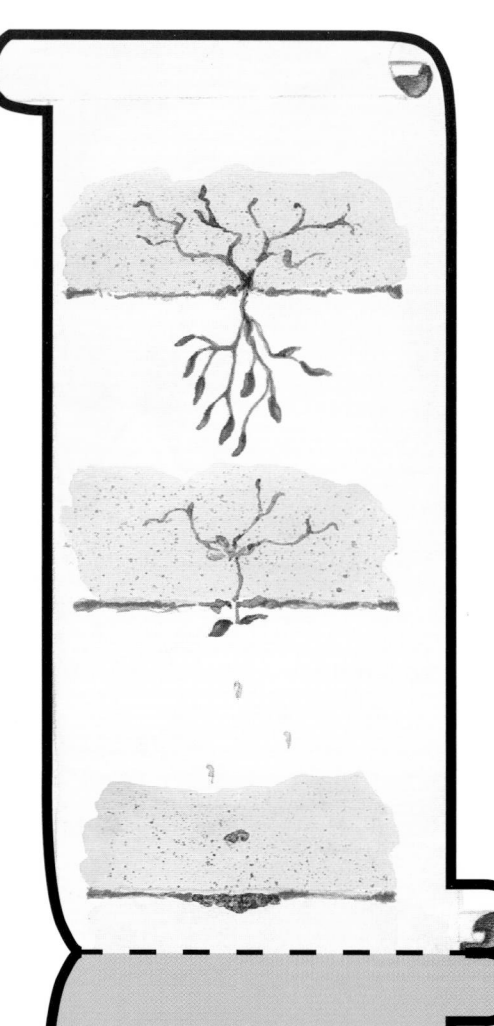

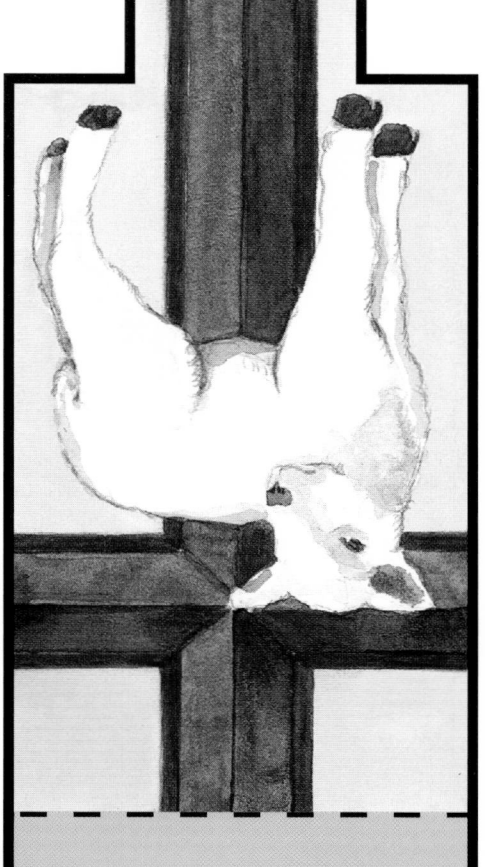

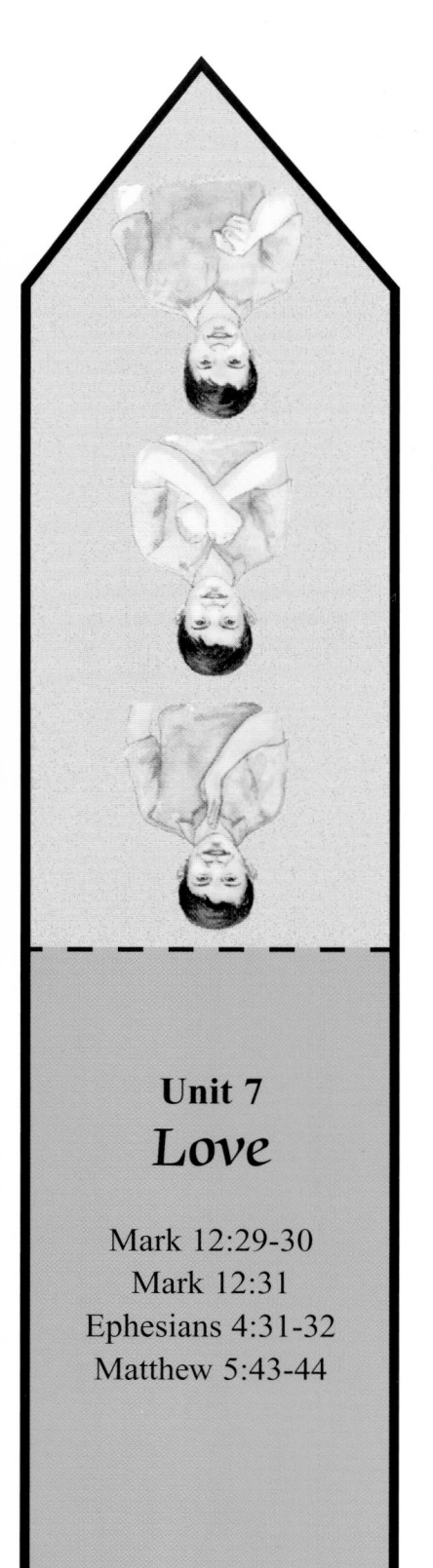

Unit 9
Christ and His People

Matthew 16:15-16
Ephesians 3:20-21
II Corinthians 9:6-7
Ephesians 2:10

Unit 8
Easter: Victory over Death

Isaiah 53:3-4
Isaiah 53:5-6

Unit 7
Love

Mark 12:29-30
Mark 12:31
Ephesians 4:31-32
Matthew 5:43-44

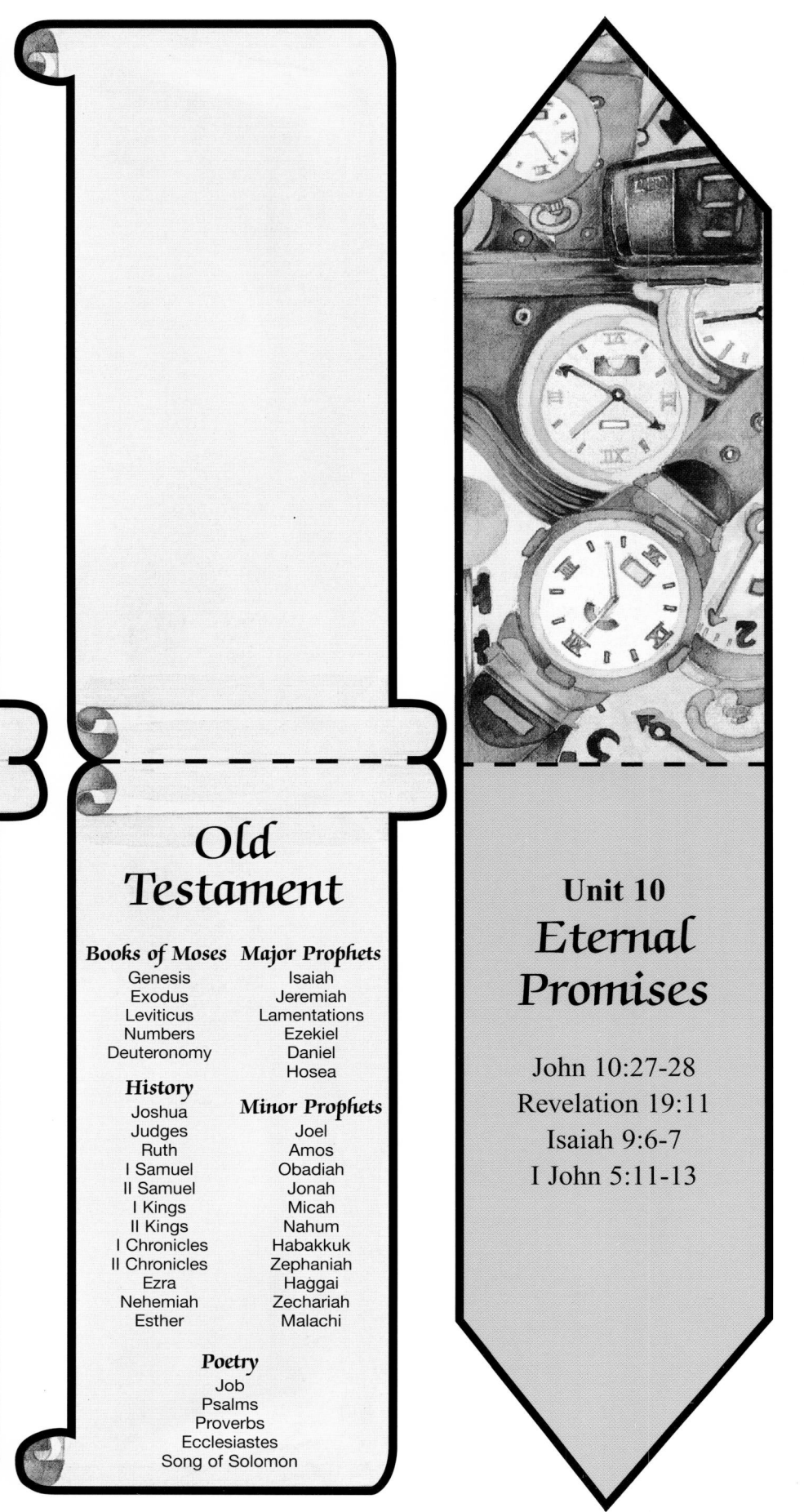

New Testament

Gospels
Matthew
Mark
Luke
John

History
Acts

Paul's Letters
Romans
I Corinthians
II Corinthians
Galatians
Ephesians
Philippians
Colossians
I Thessalonians
II Thessalonians
I Timothy
II Timothy
Titus
Philemon

General Letters
Hebrews
James
I Peter
II Peter
I John
II John
III John
Jude

Prophecy
Revelation

Old Testament

Books of Moses
Genesis
Exodus
Leviticus
Numbers
Deuteronomy

History
Joshua
Judges
Ruth
I Samuel
II Samuel
I Kings
II Kings
I Chronicles
II Chronicles
Ezra
Nehemiah
Esther

Poetry
Job
Psalms
Proverbs
Ecclesiastes
Song of Solomon

Major Prophets
Isaiah
Jeremiah
Lamentations
Ezekiel
Daniel
Hosea

Minor Prophets
Joel
Amos
Obadiah
Jonah
Micah
Nahum
Habakkuk
Zephaniah
Haggai
Zechariah
Malachi

Unit 10
Eternal Promises

John 10:27-28
Revelation 19:11
Isaiah 9:6-7
I John 5:11-13

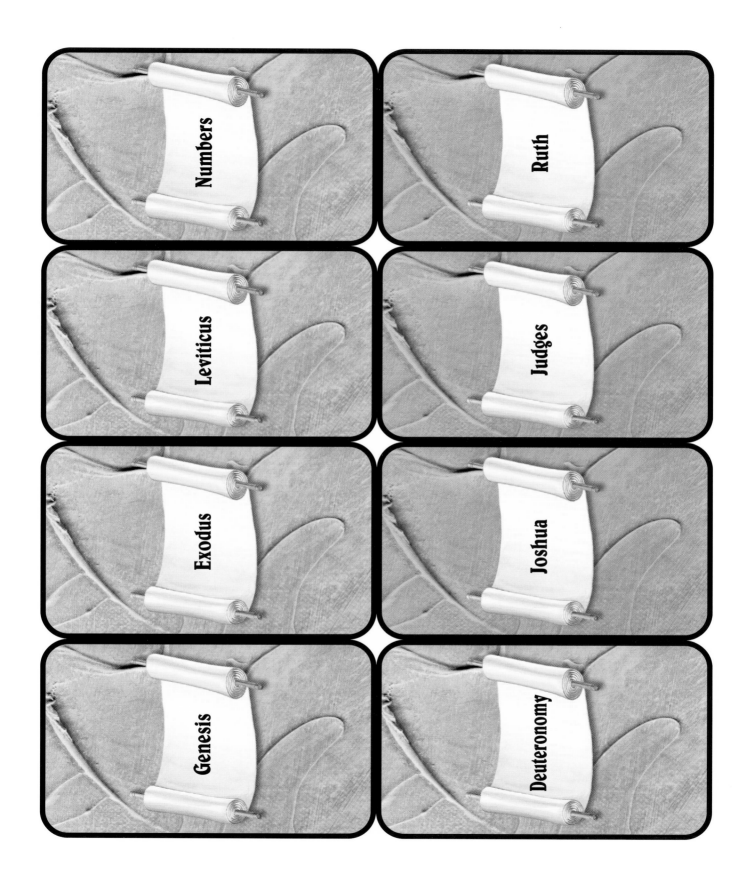

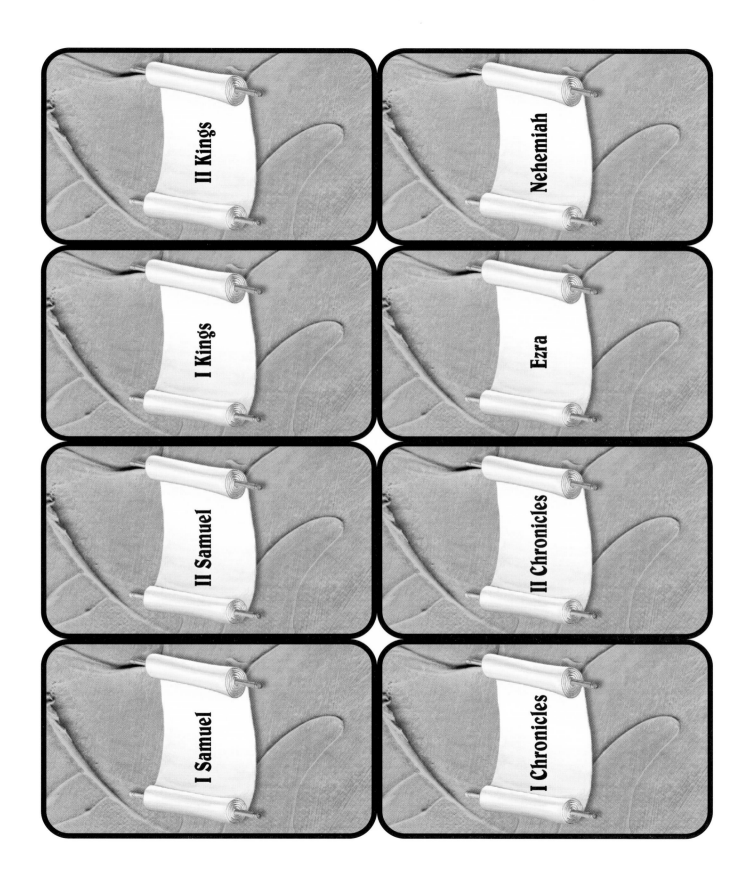

II Kings

Nehemiah

I Kings

Ezra

II Samuel

II Chronicles

I Samuel

I Chronicles

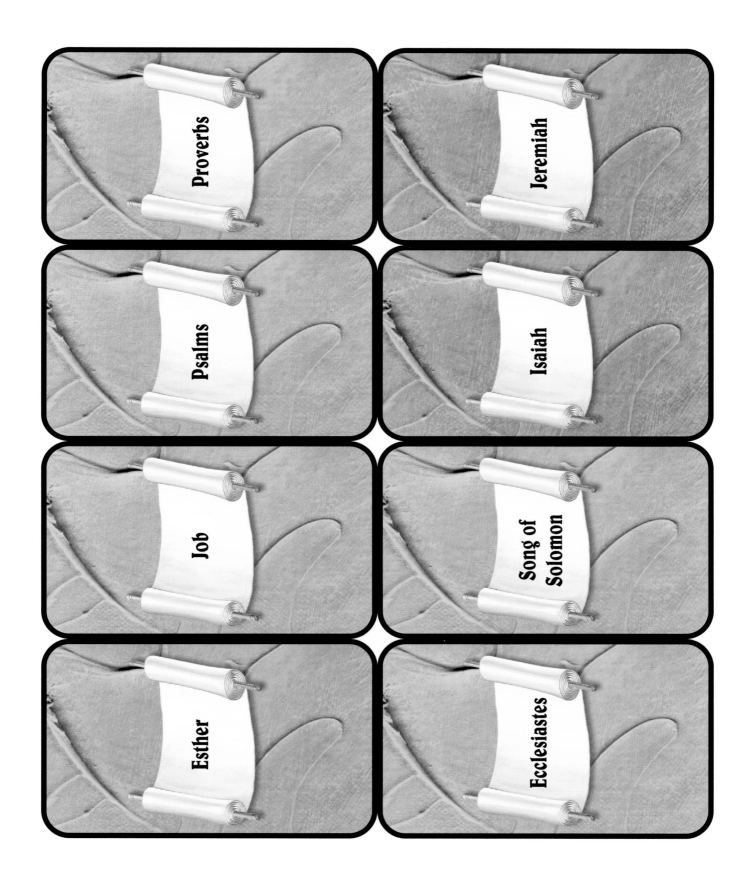

Proverbs

Jeremiah

Psalms

Isaiah

Job

Song of Solomon

Esther

Ecclesiastes

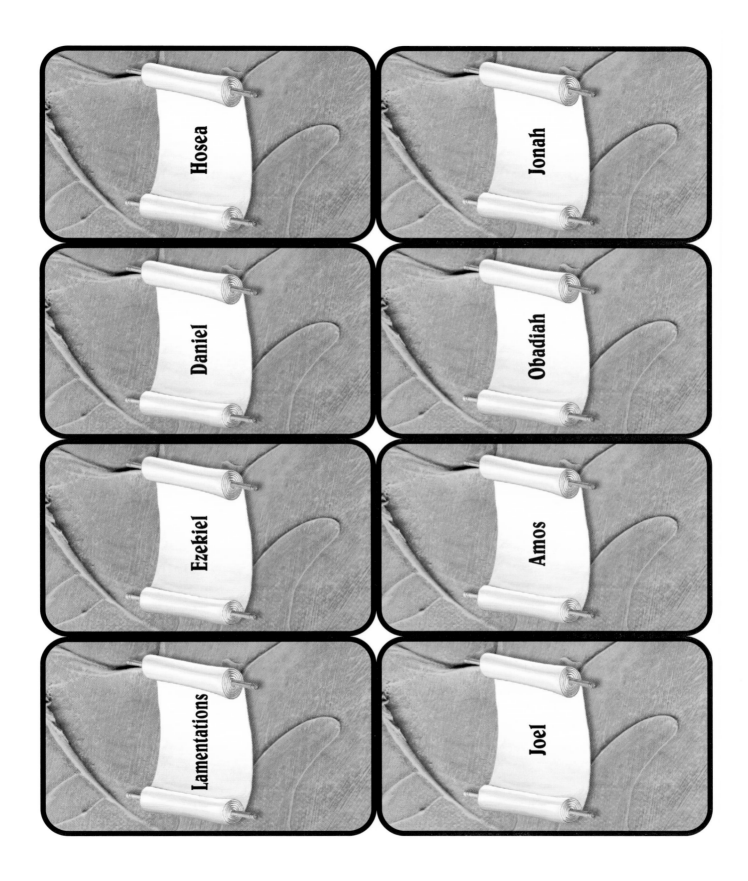

Hosea

Jonah

Daniel

Obadiah

Ezekiel

Amos

Lamentations

Joel

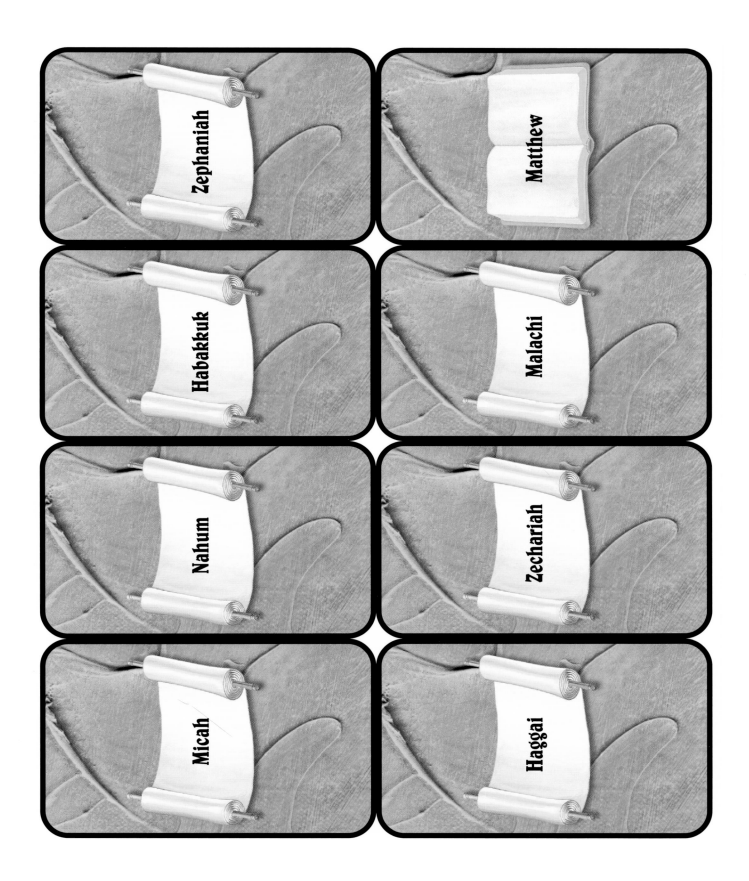

Zephaniah

Matthew

Habakkuk

Malachi

Nahum

Zechariah

Micah

Haggai

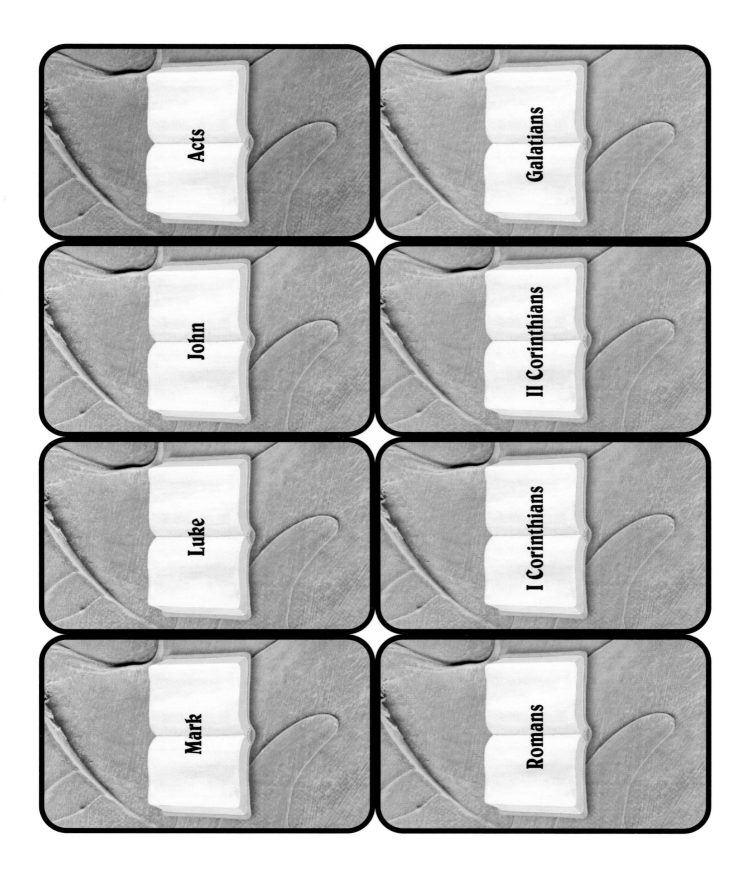

Acts

Galatians

John

II Corinthians

Luke

I Corinthians

Mark

Romans

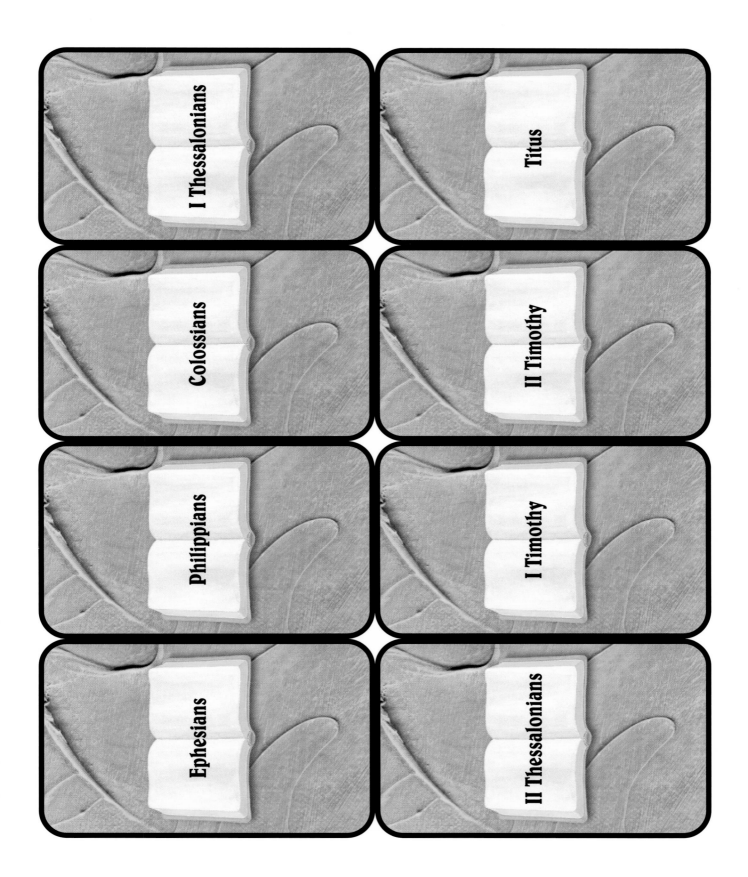

I Thessalonians

Titus

Colossians

II Timothy

Philippians

I Timothy

Ephesians

II Thessalonians

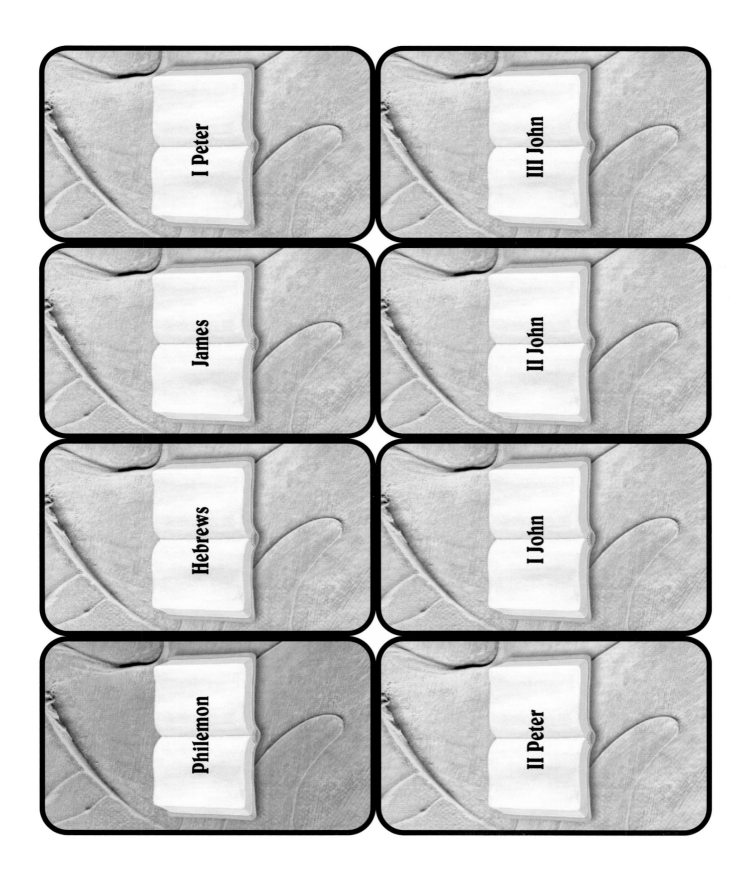

I Peter

James

Hebrews

Philemon

III John

II John

I John

II Peter

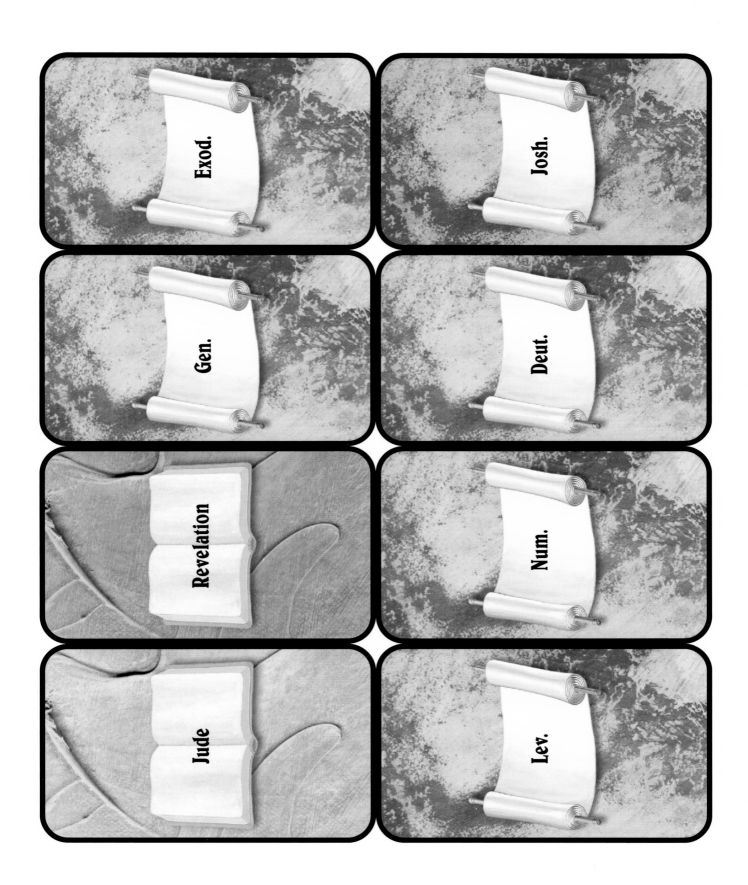

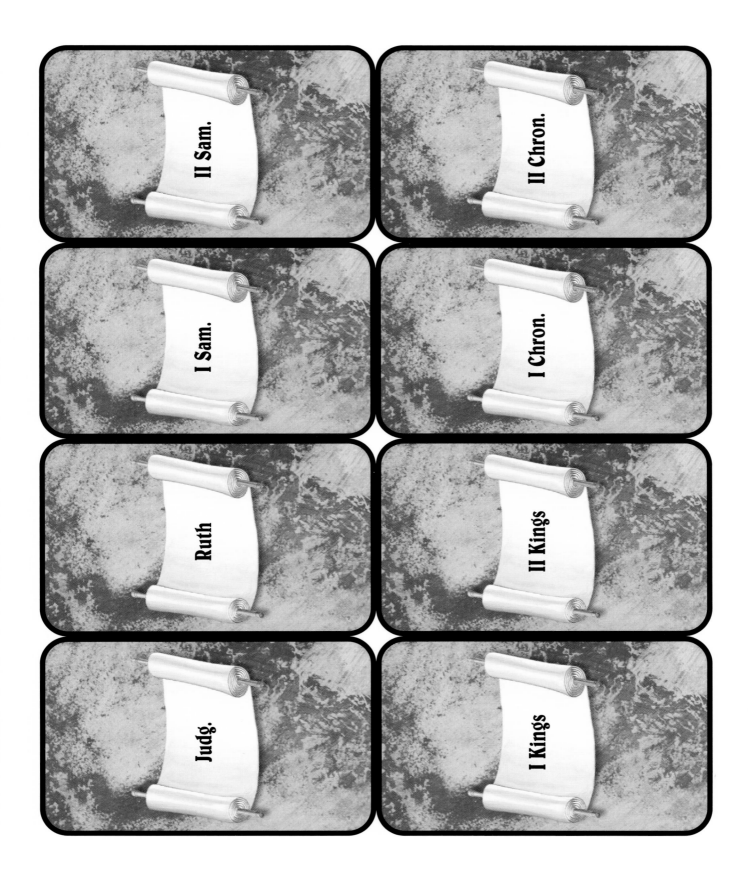

II Sam.

II Chron.

I Sam.

I Chron.

Ruth

II Kings

Judg.

I Kings

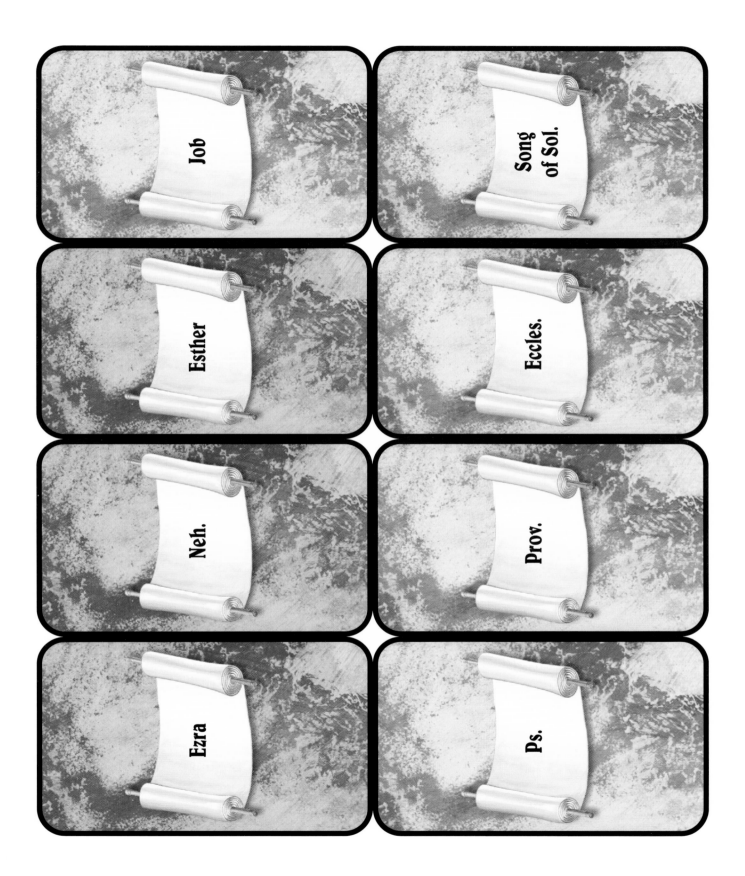

Job

Song of Sol.

Esther

Eccles.

Neh.

Prov.

Ezra

Ps.

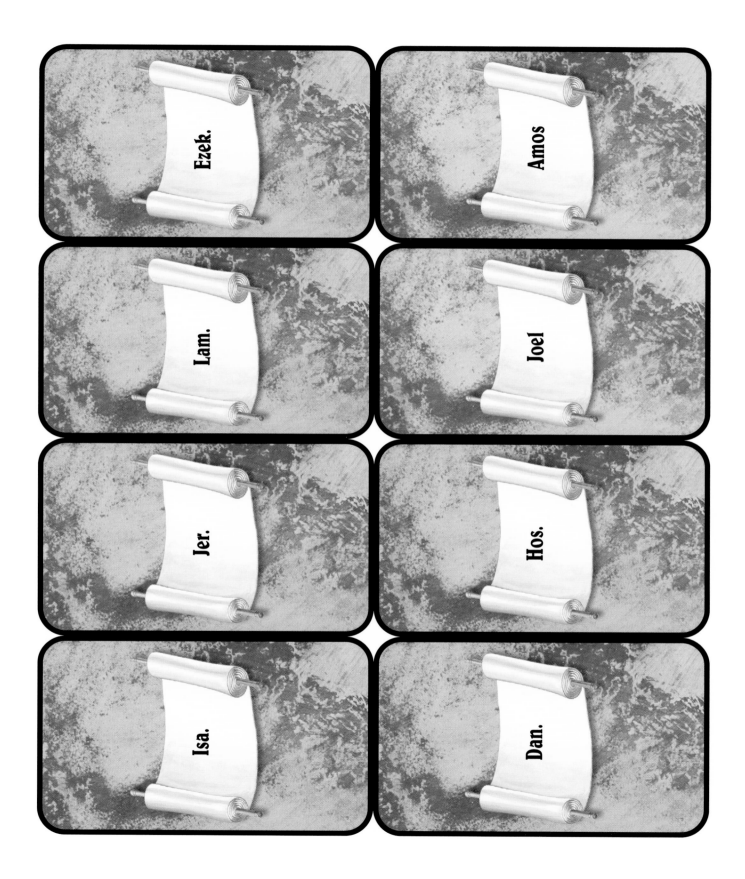

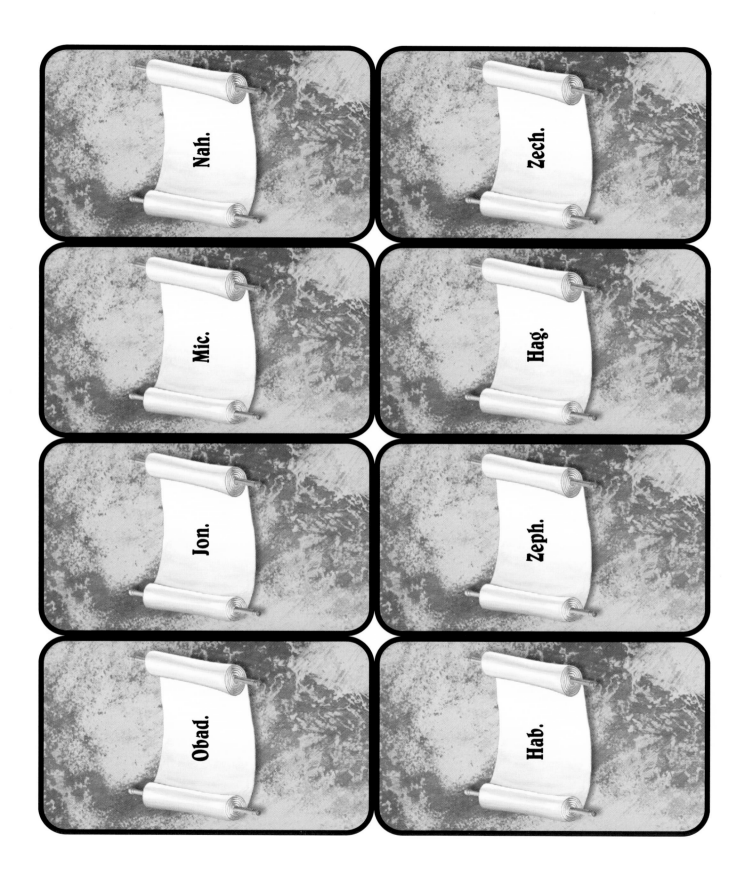

Nah.

Zech.

Mic.

Hag.

Jon.

Zeph.

Obad.

Hab.

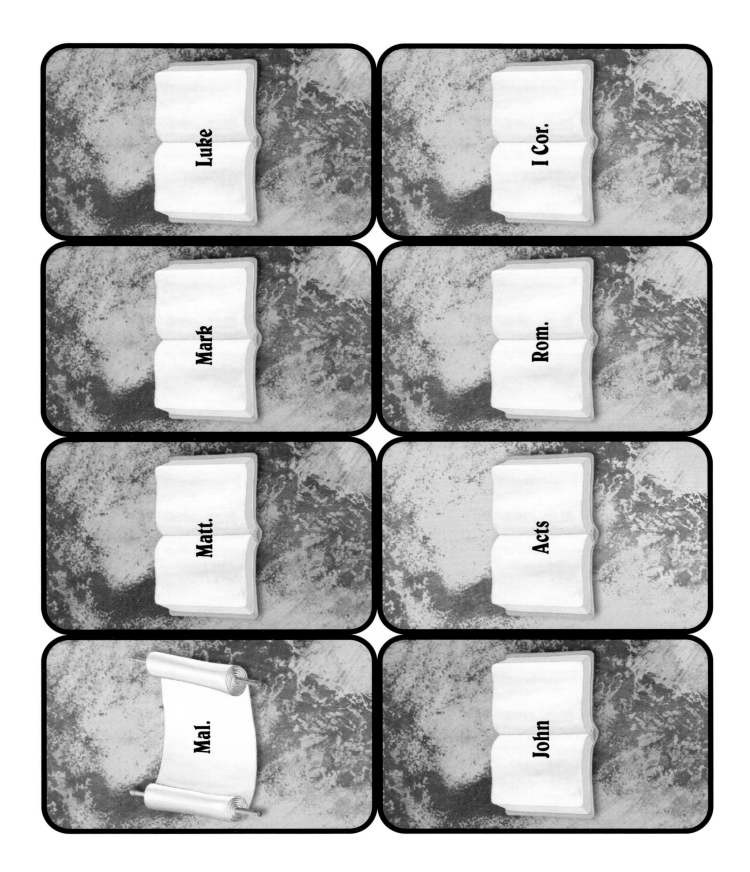

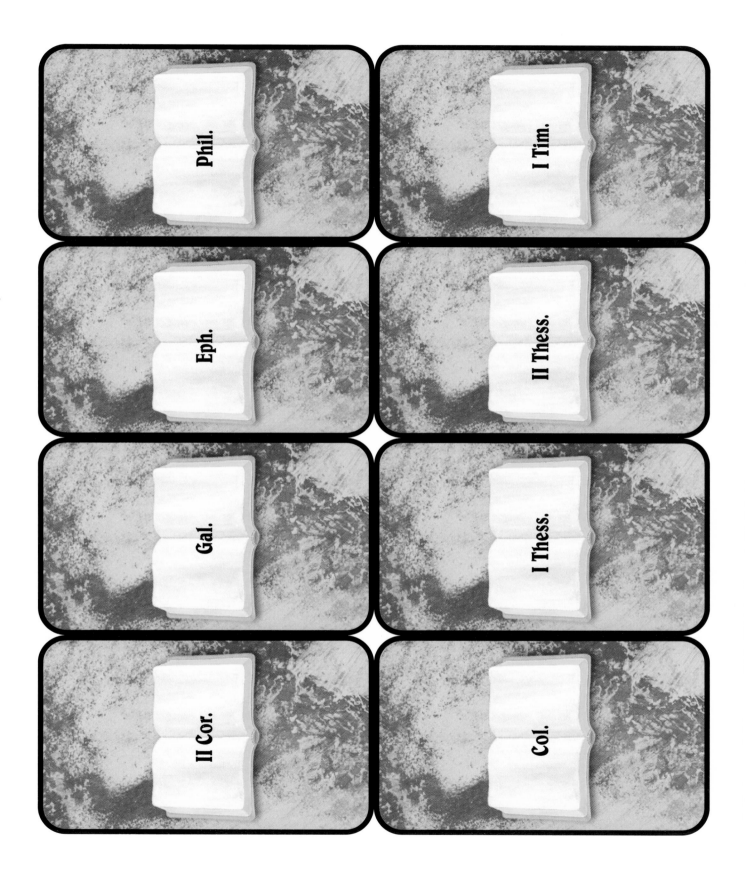

Phil.

I Tim.

Eph.

II Thess.

Gal.

I Thess.

II Cor.

Col.

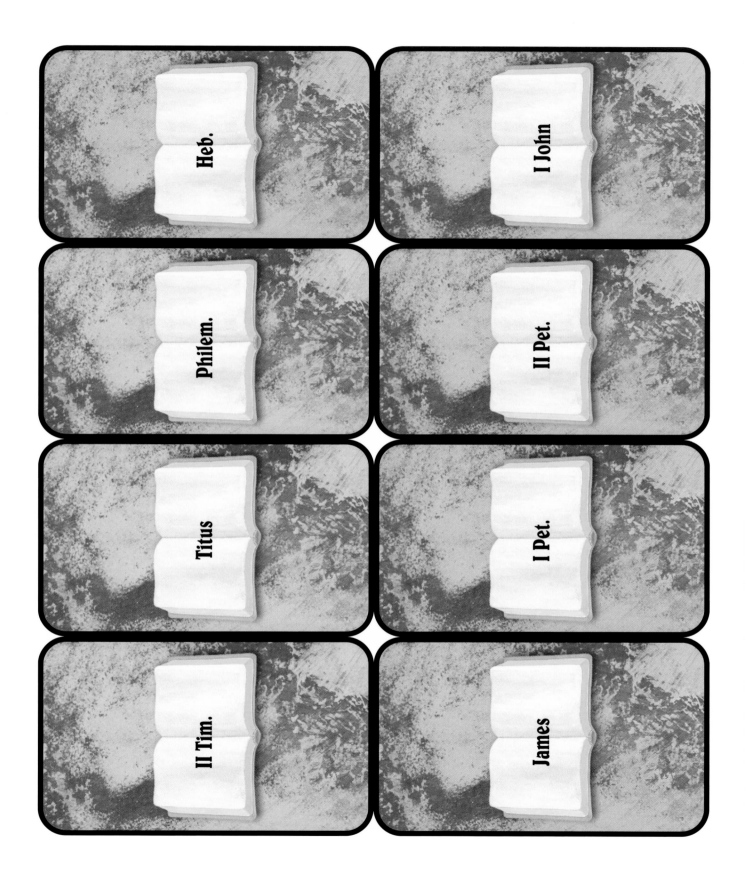